TUTOR'S

COMMUNICATION ON target

Rod and Moira Ashley

Hodder & Stoughton
LONDON SYDNEY AUCKLAND TORONTO

Contents

The publishers would like to thank the following for permission to reproduce material in this volume:
City and Guilds for the blank Individual Record Sheets.

Every effort has been made to trace and acknowledge ownership of copyright. The publishers will be glad to make suitable arrangements with any copyright holders whom it has not been possible to contact.

British Library Cataloguing in Publication Data
Ashley, Rod
Communication on target.
Teacher's book
1. Communication skills
I. Title II. Ashley, Moira
302.2
ISBN 0 340 53736 1

First published 1991

Typeset by Wearside Tradespools, Boldon, Tyne and Wear.
Printed in Great Britain for Hodder and Stoughton Educational, a division of Hodder and Stoughton Ltd, Mill Road, Dunton Green, Sevenoaks, Kent by Imediaprint, London.

Introduction

All teachers of Communication realise just how important it is to present students with work which is not only stimulating and convincing, but which also uses a realistic and wide range of source material. Experience as an Assessor for City and Guilds 361 has shown that many centres have little time to develop their own assignments or may feel diffident about so doing.

Communication On Target is published with the aim of alleviating this situation, by providing a range of assignments at three levels, across different contexts and scenarios. The variety of material at three levels (two level 1, eight level 2 and two level 3 assignments) also makes the book suitable for mixed ability teaching. Assignment 10, additionally, can be upgraded from level 2 to level 3.

The *Tutor's Guide* is intended to assist both with the administration of the assignments and also with some aspects of assessment.

These suggestions result from experience of teaching the assignments, but they are not meant to be prescriptive. Rather, they are intended to ensure the smooth running of classwork and to remind tutors of any particular facilities or equipment needed. In some cases, photocopies of materials in looseleaf form need to be supplied to students at some stage. In other cases, information needs to be made available at a particular stage of the assignment.

In the same way, the assessment hints are not prescriptive, but merely underline some aspects of assessment – or will save the tutor's time by providing a ready answer. They do not pretend to mimic the assignments set by City and Guilds (or any other body), either in close observance of format or detailed assessment criteria.

We hope that you find the materials useful and stimulating for your students. However, it is *not* the book's intention to replace but to supplement local, centre-devised assignments, tailored specifically to the needs and interests of your own students.

What is provided instead is a collection of assignments for students of varying ability and maturity. In order to complete them, they must use as wide a range of communication skills, and as much initiative as possible within the single medium of a book.

Tasks have been devised so as to be easily administered by centres that are not well equipped. However, centres which are well endowed with equipment or facilities may wish to adapt the assignments in a more suitable way, e.g. by using a video camera.

Individual record-sheet for achievement of objectives

Please use explanatory notes overleaf

CS/CW6

Candidate's name ______________ Candidate number ______________ Teacher ______________

READING

Level	Assignment Exercise	Date (CONTEXT)	1.1a	1.1b	1.1c	1.1d	1.1e	1.1f	1.1g	1.1h	1.2a	1.2b	1.2c	1.2d	1.2e	1.2f	1.3a	1.3b	1.3c
			Read and understand data								Identify statements which are are not supported by evidence within a given context						Find and use information		
	HOLIDAY ON GOWER	SOCIAL	✓	✓	✓							✓					✓		
I	A NIGHT OUT	EDUCATION	✓		✓												✓		
	FILLING THE GAP	WORK	✓	✓	✓	✓					✓	✓			✓		✓		
	OUR PLACE	SOCIAL/EDUCATION	✓	✓	✓	✓	✓				✓	✓					✓	✓	
II	SMOKE SIGNALS	EDUCATION	✓	✓	✓	✓					✓	✓			✓		✓	✓	
	GETTING THE FAX RIGHT	WORK	✓	✓	✓		✓				✓	✓	✓	✓	✓		✓		
	PUTTING IT RIGHT	SOCIAL	✓		✓		✓				✓	✓	✓		✓		✓		

LISTENING

Assignment Exercise	2.1a	2.1b	2.1c	2.1d	2.1e	2.1f	2.1g	2.1h	2.2a	2.2b	2.2c	2.2d	2.2e	2.2f
	Listen to and understand information in oral form								Identify statements which are are not supported by evidence within a given context					
HOLIDAY ON GOWER	✓		✓											
A NIGHT OUT	✓		✓						✓	✓				
FILLING THE GAP	✓	✓	✓	✓		✓			✓	✓	✓	✓	✓	
OUR PLACE			✓	✓		✓								
SMOKE SIGNALS	✓	✓	✓	✓	✓	✓			✓	✓	✓	✓	✓	
GETTING THE FAX RIGHT	✓	✓	✓	✓	✓	✓			✓	✓	✓	✓	✓	
PUTTING IT RIGHT	✓	✓	✓							✓				

WRITING

Assignment Exercise	3.1a	3.1b	3.1c	3.1d	3.1e	3.1f	3.1g	3.1h	3.1i	3.1j	3.2a	3.2b	3.2c	3.2d	3.2e
	Organise content and write effectively										Use tabular and graphical material effectively				
HOLIDAY ON GOWER	✓	✓	✓	✓								✓			
A NIGHT OUT	✓		✓	✓											
FILLING THE GAP	✓	✓	✓	✓		✓	✓	✓	✓						
OUR PLACE	✓	✓	✓		✓	✓	✓	✓				✓	✓		
SMOKE SIGNALS	✓	✓	✓			✓	✓	✓	✓		✓	✓	✓		
GETTING THE FAX RIGHT	✓	✓	✓	✓		✓	✓	✓			✓				
PUTTING IT RIGHT	✓	✓	✓	✓		✓	✓	✓							

SPEAKING

Assignment Exercise	4.1a	4.1b	4.1c	4.1d	4.1e	4.1f	4.1g	4.2a	4.2b	4.2c	4.2d
	Organise content and communicate effectively							Express tabular and graphical data in oral form			
HOLIDAY ON GOWER	✓	✓	✓								
A NIGHT OUT	✓	✓	✓								
FILLING THE GAP	✓	✓	✓	✓	✓						
OUR PLACE	✓	✓	✓	✓							
SMOKE SIGNALS	✓	✓	✓	✓	✓	✓		✓	✓		
GETTING THE FAX RIGHT	✓		✓	✓		✓					
PUTTING IT RIGHT	✓	✓	✓	✓	✓	✓					

Key: ☐ objectives assessed at levels I, II, III; (light shading) objectives assessed at levels II and III only; (dark shading) = objectives assessed at level III only

Individual record-sheet for achievement of objectives

Please use explanatory notes overleaf

CS CW6

Candidate's name ______________ Candidate number ______________ Teacher ______________

READING — 1.1 Read and understand data; 1.2 Identify statements which are are not supported by evidence within a given context; 1.3 Find and use infor-mation

Level	Assignment Exercise	Date	1.1a	1.1b	1.1c	1.1d	1.1e	1.1f	1.1g	1.1h	1.2a	1.2b	1.2c	1.2d	1.2e	1.2f	1.3a	1.3b	1.3c
II	A SOUND DECISION ?	SOCIAL	✓	✓	✓	✓						✓					✓	✓	
	MAKING YOUR MARK	WORK	✓		✓		✓				✓	✓	✓	✓	✓		✓		
	UP TO YOUR EARS	WORK	✓		✓		✓										✓	✓	
	RIGHT PRICE RECORDS	WORK	✓	✓	✓	✓	✓	✓		✓	✓	✓	✓		✓	✓	✓	✓	
III	WELL WISHERS	WORK	✓	✓	✓	✓	✓	✓	✓	✓		✓			✓	✓	✓		✓

LISTENING — 2.1 Listen to and understand information in oral form; 2.2 Identify statements which are are not supported by evidence within a given context

Level	Assignment Exercise	Date	2.1a	2.1b	2.1c	2.1d	2.1e	2.1f	2.1g	2.1h	2.2a	2.2b	2.2c	2.2d	2.2e	2.2f
II	A SOUND DECISION ?	SOCIAL	✓		✓	✓	✓	✓				✓	✓		✓	
	MAKING YOUR MARK	WORK	✓	✓	✓	✓	✓	✓			✓	✓	✓	✓	✓	
	UP TO YOUR EARS	WORK	✓	✓	✓	✓	✓	✓							✓	
	RIGHT PRICE RECORDS	WORK	✓	✓	✓	✓	✓	✓	✓	✓	✓	✓	✓	✓		✓
III	WELL WISHERS	WORK	✓		✓	✓	✓		✓	✓		✓			✓	✓

WRITING — 3.1 Organise content and write effectively; 3.2 Use tabular and graphical material effectively

Level	Assignment Exercise	Date	3.1a	3.1b	3.1c	3.1d	3.1e	3.1f	3.1g	3.1h	3.1i	3.1j	3.2a	3.2b	3.2c	3.2d	3.2e
II	A SOUND DECISION ?	SOCIAL	✓		✓		✓		✓	✓							
	MAKING YOUR MARK	WORK	✓	✓	✓		✓	✓	✓	✓	✓						
	UP TO YOUR EARS	WORK	✓	✓	✓	✓	✓	✓	✓	✓	✓		✓	✓	✓		
	RIGHT PRICE RECORDS	WORK	✓	✓	✓	✓		✓	✓	✓	✓	✓	✓		✓	✓	✓
III	WELL WISHERS	WORK	✓	✓	✓			✓	✓	✓	✓	✓	✓	✓	✓	✓	✓

SPEAKING — 4.1 Organise content and communicate effectively; 4.2 Express tabular and graphical data in oral form

Level	Assignment Exercise	Date	4.1a	4.1b	4.1c	4.1d	4.1e	4.1f	4.1g	4.2a	4.2b	4.2c	4.2d
II	A SOUND DECISION ?	SOCIAL	✓	✓	✓	✓	✓			✓	✓		
	MAKING YOUR MARK	WORK	✓	✓	✓	✓	✓	✓					
	UP TO YOUR EARS	WORK	✓	✓	✓	✓	✓	✓					
	RIGHT PRICE RECORDS	WORK	✓	✓	✓	✓			✓	✓	✓	✓	✓
III	WELL WISHERS	WORK	✓	✓	✓	✓	✓	✓	✓	✓	✓	✓	✓

Key: ☐ = objectives assessed at levels I, II, III; light shading = objectives assessed at levels II and III only; dark shading = objectives assessed at level III only

ASSIGNMENT 1

Holiday on Gower

This assignment will probably be the first one attempted for most candidates, and it should give them a flavour of the practical, problem solving nature of the assignments.

Students need to practise giving clear instructions to others. This could start simply with the communication of such an instruction from their own classroom to another part of the establishment. However, it would be useful to organise some preliminary practice with motorists' directions. Younger students, in particular, forget that they cannot direct vehicles the wrong way up one-way streets, etc!

Students should be issued with a copy of the area map (document 3) at the outset of the assignment, to give them a sense of place. They may need to annotate it, so ensure that the copy is clear.

Task 1 The only site meeting all criteria is Eastmore Farm, Llanrhidian.

Task 2 Ensure that a telephone dialling code booklet or phone directory is available. The correct code (at time of printing) is 0792.

Task 3 A suitable range of maps should be available. Obviously, students living near the area in question will need less background material but could be encouraged to go into greater detail in their instructions.

Task 4 Any of the trekking centres is suitable. For windsurfing: Gower Promotions is only open until 30 October, so check the date booked. No operational dates are given for Sailsports, but Mumbles is less convenient.

Tape transcript

Hello, and thank you for phoning to book your Gower camping holiday. I'm afraid that there's no-one here at the moment to take your booking personally.

However, you can book by leaving the following information. Please have a pen and paper ready to jot down anything you need before the tone sounds. Please give:

- Your name and address
- Your telephone number, including the STD code
- The number of nights and the dates you wish to book
- The number of tents
- The number of vehicles
- The registration numbers of vehicles
- And, the number of pets you may be bringing

Thank you for booking with us.

Please speak after the tone.

Area map of Gower

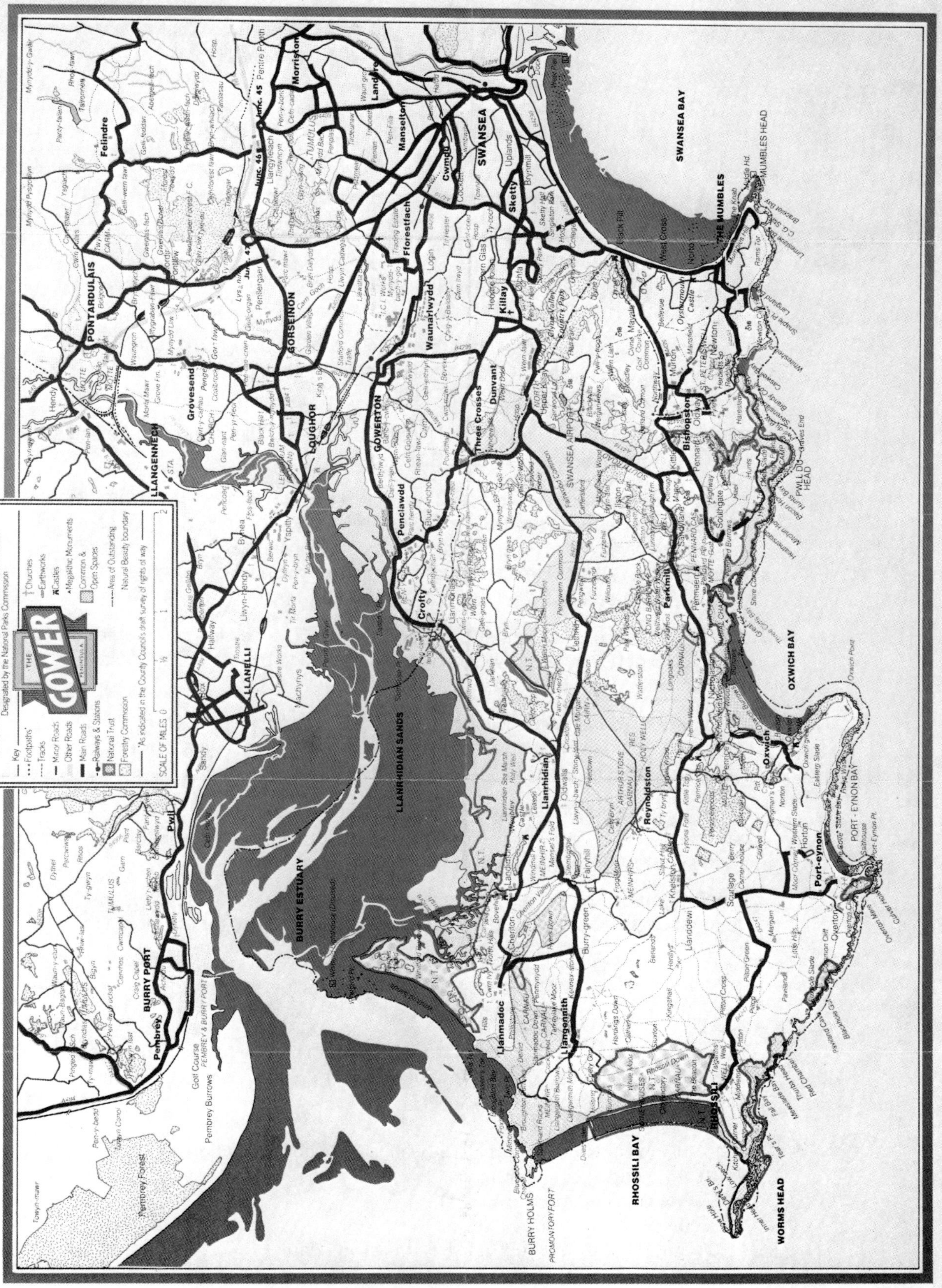

ASSIGNMENT 2

A Night on the Town

Task 1

Transcript of local radio show

And now, let's take a look backstage at our local theatres to see what's in store for you during November.

Well, for all you opera buffs, the Grand in Seaton is playing host to the Welsh National Opera for a week – plenty of passion and colour in their ever-popular productions.

Later at the Grand, an unusual but highly acclaimed ballet about the life and work of that 'Matchstick Man' artist, L. S. Lowry.

And if all that sounds a bit too highbrow, how about two plays which are being staged at the Little Theatre? One is an Alan Ayckbourn comedy which I am told had them rolling in the aisles. The other is equally hilarious – *The Tart and the Vicar's Wife*. But be warned, though: the subject mightn't go down too well with your grandparents!

The Civic Centre, Port Tennant, is the setting for 'The Ken Dodd Laughter Show'. And you'd better book early if you want to be tickled by this ever-popular comedian.

Also at Port Tennant, you'll find an enjoyable night out for 'The Good Old Days', featuring a variety of musical acts, as well as comedians, a ventriloquist and a host of other entertainers.

Lastly, Colbourne Theatre. Now here you'll find two different types of entertainment. There's the Winton Jazz Orchestra and a play called *Lend Me a Tenor* (very original, apparently). Well, I'm all for originality.

Oh, Colbourne Theatre also ask me to remind you that because of extensive renovation work, the ground floor toilets will be out of use for the month of November.

Well, that's it for now, folks – see your local press for details and make sure *you* get out and support your local theatres.

After listening to the broadcast, students should be able to discount all events at the Colbourne Theatre (toilets out of use) and *The Tart and the Vicar's Wife* (unsuitable content).

Task 2

The only event which meets all the criteria is 'The Good Old Days'.

Reasons for rejecting others:

- Colbourne Theatre (see task 1);
- 'A Simple Man': wrong dates;
- Opera: the only one in English is the wrong date;
- Ken Dodd: wrong date;
- *The Tart and the Vicar's Wife* (see task 1);
- *Chorus of Disapproval*: too expensive.

Task 3

Ensure that all necessary information is included, i.e. name and venue of performance, date, number of seats required (25). NB There is a choice of circle or stalls – the latter being more suitable for the elderly.

Task 4

Ansafone tape transcript

Hello. Thank you for calling Weaver's Coaches. I'm sorry that no one is here at the moment to take your call.

If you would like to make a coach booking, please speak after the tone, leaving details of the booking you wish to make. Don't forget to leave your name and telephone number so that we can get back to you to confirm your booking.

Ensure that the message gives the following information:
- size of coach required (29-seater);
- date required;
- pick-up time* and pick-up point;
- pick-up time from theatre*;
- student's name and college phone number.

*Students have been told to allow 45 minutes journey time. Some may decide to allow more time.

ASSIGNMENT 3

Filling the Gap

Task 1 Transcript – extract from radio 'Food Programme'

GUEST ... to your third point, I mean, to say that chocolate's bad for you is simply absurd. There's absolutely no evidence that sugar is harmful to health; and chocolate does, in fact, supply us with energy in a very direct way, as well as contributing significantly to the protein intake which the body requires.

INTERVIEWER Perhaps I could interrupt, Mr Bauer? We could go on arguing all day about the value, or otherwise, of chocolate. It's certainly true to say that whatever chocolate does to us, we in Britain eat a vast amount of it! Can you give us a picture of *why* we eat it?

GUEST *Why* do we eat chocolate? Well, that's very simple – we enjoy it! You know, there's no other industry in the world that gives so much pleasure to so many people as the confectionery industry ...

INTERVIEWER (*interrupting*) Oh, that's a rather extravagant claim, surely! But leaving that aside, can you tell us *when* we buy it?

GUEST Well – giving chocolate is associated with all our happy, festive occasions: Christmas, Easter, Mother's Day. We give chocolate to say 'Thank you' or 'Congratulations' or 'I love you'. On a more down-to-earth note, we buy it when we want a nutritious, tasty snack.

INTERVIEWER Could you tell us, perhaps, something more about the people who *buy* chocolate. For instance, do you know if men or women have the sweeter tooth?

GUEST Well, let me give you a breakdown of chocolate buying habits in the UK. We eat, on average, about 250 grams per head per week. Now surprisingly, that level has remained constant over the last 25 years. Most chocolate – by that I mean about 60% – is bought by women: for themselves and their families. Then about 27% is bought by men, and roughly 13% by children up to the age of 15 ...

INTERVIEWER (*interrupting*) I'm sorry to bring you to a rapid halt there, Mr Bauer, but we've come to the end of our time. Thank you very much for coming along.

On Debonair, it's time for a commercial break. After the break, bottled water – is it really better for us, or is it just money down the drain?

Students should take notes about buying habits. They should be able to distinguish between factual information and biased comment from Mr Bauer.

Task 2

A very open-ended task. Look for originality in name and, preferably, some nautical connection.

Task 3

Very open-ended. Group should be able to reject tactfully and justify their final choice, by measuring it against the following criteria – Schooner connection and youth appeal.

Task 4

Letter should have appropriate layout and contain relevant material.

ASSIGNMENT 4

Our Place

This assignment is more open-ended than some of the others. In order to devise an information leaflet about their own locality, students will need access to outside bodies by post, phone, or – preferably – by visiting them in person. This is also true for task 4: the talking map. Students will need the opportunity to explore locations thoroughly, in order to create an interesting tape.

Both tasks 1 and 4 are group activities. The other tasks are individual ones. Wherever group tasks operate, assessment is more complex than the assessing of individual performance. In tasks 1 and 4, here, the skills being fostered are:

- making an individual contribution to group effort;
- playing specific role(s) in division of labour;
- aiding positive teamwork;
- ability to meet deadlines set by rest of group;
- being supportive of others' suggestions and efforts.

Students will obviously respond differently to these demands and should therefore be assessed individually for their contributions to group product and process.

Task 1 Reference books, such as those mentioned, need to be available in class.

Task 2 It may be preferable for students to base this task on their own hall.

Task 3 The order form is printed below for photocopying.

D & A Cash and Carry

ORDER FORM

From: ....

....

Item	No. req'd	Unit Price	Total Cost	VAT
		Sub total		
		5% discount (where applicable)		
		TOTAL		

Task 4 Students should be assessed on *how* they present the information – so it should not matter if several groups select the same location.

ASSIGNMENT 5

Smoke Signals . . .

Task 1 The two questionnaires are printed below for photocopying.

SMOKERS' QUESTIONNAIRE

1 How many cigarettes do you smoke a day?

under 5 ☐ 6–10 ☐ 11–20 ☐ over 20 ☐

2 When did you first start smoking? ....

3 Why did you have your first cigarette? ....

4 Indicate whether you agree or disagree with

Smoking is . . .	Agree	Disagree
grown up	☐	☐
sophisticated	☐	☐
cool	☐	☐
sexy	☐	☐
relaxing	☐	☐
fun	☐	☐

5 Do you think it is safe to smoke low-tar cigarettes? Y/N

6 What % of people in the UK are smokers?

23% ☐ 34% ☐ 62% ☐ 75% ☐*

7 Do you suffer from coughs, chestiness or breathlessness? Y/N

8 Have you ever tried to give up smoking? Y/N

9 If so, what made you start smoking again? ....

10 If someone at work or in the same room as you complained about your smoking, would you –

put out your cigarette ☐
move away from them ☐
ignore them ☐
defend your right to smoke ☐

11 Did you know that your cigarette smoke is harmful to non-smokers in the same room as you? Y/N

* Answer 34%

NON-SMOKERS' QUESTIONNAIRE

1 Have you ever smoked? Y/N

2 If so (a) what made you give up? ....
(b) what helped you give up? ....
(c) what made it difficult to give up? ....

3 If you have never smoked, have you ever felt under any pressure to start? Y/N

4 Which of the following statements do you think explains why people smoke?

Smoking is . . .
grown-up ☐
sophisticated ☐
cool ☐
sexy ☐
relaxing ☐
fun ☐

5 Does other people's smoking annoy you? Y/N

6 If so, what do you do about it?

complain to them ☐
avoid them or the place where they smoke ☐
put up with it ☐

7 Do you know that breathing cigarette smoke is harmful to non-smokers? Y/N

8 What % of people in the UK are smokers

23% ☐ 34% ☐ 62% ☐ 75%* ☐

*Answer 34%

Task 2 Depending on the number of students, this might be done in larger groups.

Task 3 Obviously, the choices here are dependent upon centre resources. Assessment should take account of the amount of time taken and the relative complexity of the medium selected.

Task 4 Students will by now be familiar with many of the arguments on both sides. Assessment should take into account the sensitivity shown to others' feelings. Although a lively debate should emerge, students must be aware that a *rational* discussion is paramount.

ASSIGNMENT 6

Getting the Fax Right

Whilst a definition of facsimile machines is given, a brief introduction explaining their prevalence in business today would be useful. Headed notepaper, order forms, and *Yellow Pages* should provide plenty of examples.

Task 1 AD200 is only one to meet all criteria.

Task 2 Groups of three or four students should be formed. Plenty of scope for discussion of style. Letter 2 is the most appropriate, but credit should be given for devising a better alternative.

Task 3 **Tape transcript**

CHRIS Hello, Kim – it's Chris from Despatch, here. Can you do us a favour?

KIM Yes, all right – what do you want?

CHRIS I've got details of next Tuesday's and Wednesday's deliveries, but I haven't had time to sort a schedule yet and I'm off on a training course to learn how to use this fax. Can you organise the schedules, please? Remember that we can make *one morning* and *up to two afternoon* deliveries each day.

KIM Right, fine, no problem. Have you got a list of the deliveries to be made?

CHRIS Yes, I'll go slowly. Bonds require a Tuesday afternoon delivery. Got that? Tuesday afternoon for Bonds. It's a small load.

Carters need theirs by Wednesday morning, at the latest.

Dunns, a new customer, say any time Tuesday or Wednesday will suit them – morning or afternoon.

KIM Right, is that double 'n'?

CHRIS Yes – 'D.U.N.N.S.' Now, here's a couple of tricky ones: we've a small load for Edwards, but it's really delicate equipment so we've got to make it the first delivery on either day. Have you got that?

KIM Yeah, all right – we'll make that one top priority.

CHRIS Lastly, Arnolds, it's a big load – so it looks as if it can only be split with the delivery for *either* Bonds *or* Edwards, OK? That's an Arnolds/Bonds same day delivery *or* an Arnolds/Edwards.

KIM Got it.

CHRIS Thanks a lot, Kim – I'm sure you'll sort it out fine.

Task 4 Students will need a copy of the sketch map. Sequence of deliveries is:
- Tuesday: a.m. – Dunns; p.m. – Bonds, Carters *or* Carters, Bonds.
- Wednesday: a.m. – Edwards; p.m. – Arnolds.

Sketch map of delivery route

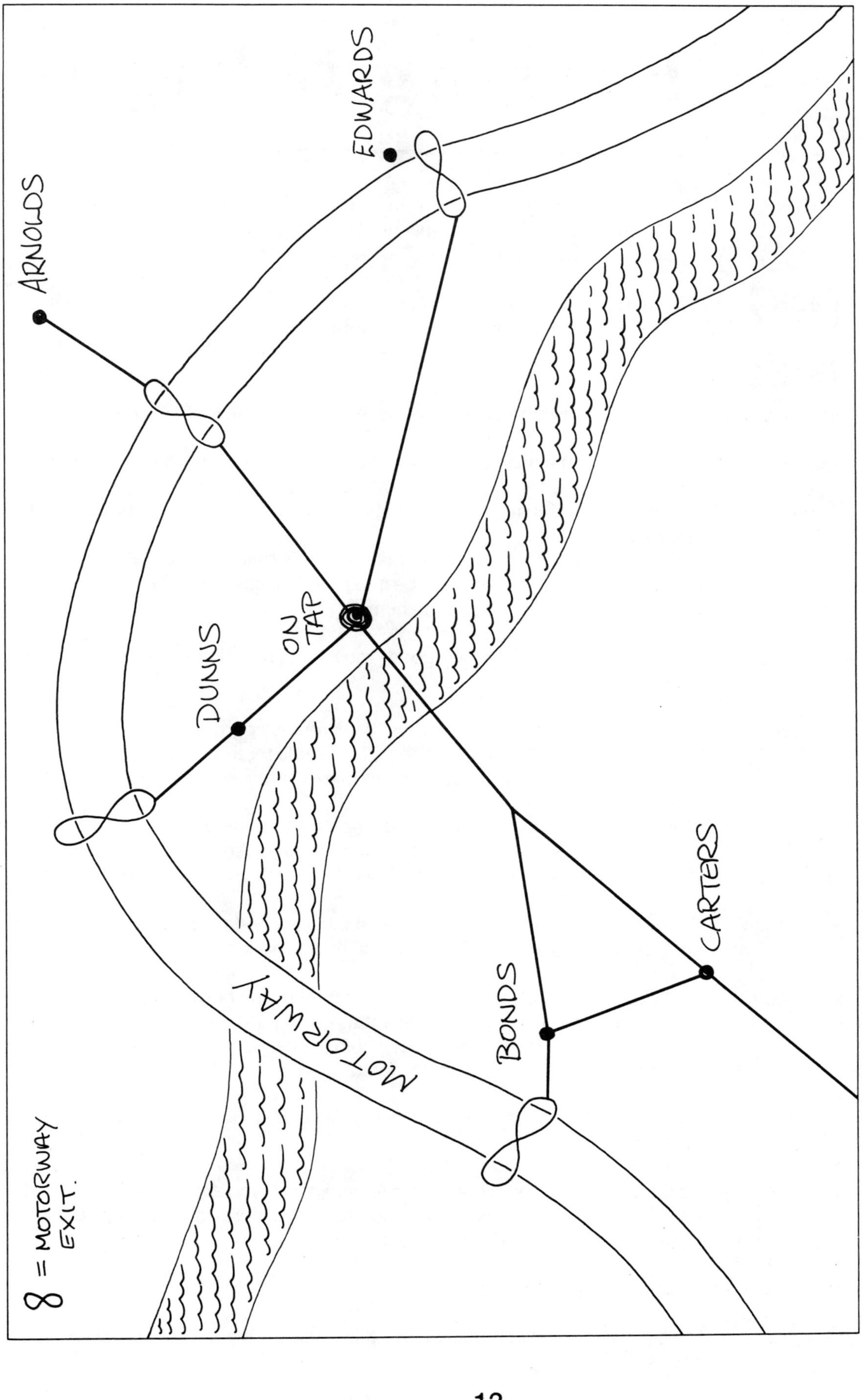

ASSIGNMENT 7

Putting it Right

Students are frequently unsure of their rights when buying goods or services. This assignment should help dispel doubts and myths. A useful introduction would be to discuss problems experienced by your own students.

Task 1 If your library stocks copies of *Which?*, it would be helpful for students to be familiar with its aims of impartiality in testing products and services.

Task 2 **Radio transcript**

INTERVIEWER Could you explain the Sale of Goods Act to us please, Mrs Todd?

MRS TODD Well, basically it's this: whenever you buy goods from a business – whether from a shop, or a catalogue, or *via* mail order, you enter into a contract with the seller. He or she must provide you with goods which meet *three* basic standards.

The first is that they must be of merchantable quality – in other words, of a quality *worth* selling. They must be free from faults, and be able to do the job you would reasonably expect of them.

INTERVIEWER Right, that's fairly clear now – goods must be of a quality worth selling. What else?

MRS TODD Well, the next point is that they must be *fit for their purpose.* For example, if you buy a tin of polish that states on the lid, 'suitable for all types of wood and leather', but you discover that it leaves streaky marks on your leather settee, then that polish is not fit for its purpose.

Thirdly, goods must *match the description* you were given. Another example: If you send away for a grey leather jacket, as advertised in a catalogue. Well you receive a black one, and that jacket clearly does not match the description.

INTERVIEWER So, what can I do if the article I have bought is *not* of a quality worth selling, or is not fit for its purpose, or does not meet its description?

MRS TODD Well you have two choices. You can either reject the goods and get a full refund. Now to do this, you should act as quickly as possible, since you could be refused a refund if you don't act within a reasonable time. The best advice is to act as soon as you discover the fault.

INTERVIEWER Some shops will persuade you to accept an exchange or a credit note, rather than offer a refund.

MRS TODD Yes, that's true, but you don't have to accept it. If you are entitled to a refund you can *insist* on one. You may, of course, find it more convenient to ask for a replacement article from the same store.

INTERVIEWER And the alternative to a refund?

MRS TODD Well, you can claim compensation – this is usually the cost of any repair necessary.

INTERVIEWER Thank you, Mrs Todd. We're going to have to stop there. I'm sure you've helped us understand more clearly what our rights are when we buy goods.

Next week, we look at your rights as a patient. Do we get 'just what the doctor ordered'?

Task 3

Role-play. The individual roles should be clarified (see below). Suitable space should be found for role-playing this standing up.

The main purpose of this task is to use the techniques and advice given by *Which?* in order to achieve a successful outcome to the exchange. Students should be encouraged towards this result.

Specifically, students in the four different roles should seek to attain the following:

Complainant: Controlled firmness and a clear explanation both of the problem and what action is required.

Shop assistant: Positive attitude, seeking to gain the full facts with tact. No rash promises.

Observers: **1** Paying careful attention to the language used by both partners. Giving positive feedback and suggestions for alternative phrasing/strategies.
2 Paying careful attention to the body language used. Positive feedback on stances adopted and any distracting mannerisms.

Students should be made aware of these objectives in simple language. In particular, the role of the observers should be stressed – it is not a passive, easy role, but one requiring concentration, sympathy and encouraging feedback.

Task 4

The letter should be appropriately laid out, and adopt a suitable tone.

ASSIGNMENT 8

A Sound Decision?

The theme of this assignment – borrowing on credit – is one which should provoke healthy discussion amongst students. The assignment will provide a vehicle for students to explore their own and others' views on credit agreements.

Some students, old enough to do so, may have taken out a credit agreement and be willing to discuss their experiences of this as an introduction.

As the assignment states, students should feel able to express their own views, and those of the role they adopt. No student should be pressurised into taking a decision which he or she is not happy with.

Students might find it illuminating to research loan and credit facilities and charges from banks, building societies, credit card companies, HP companies, etc. Any suitable material could then be used as part of the assignment.

Task 1

At the time of writing, the National & Provincial Building Society telephone helplines are available on 0898 numbers, chargeable at the standard 45p or 34p per minute rate for such calls.

The numbers are:

– buying on credit: 0898 334 156;
– borrowing (where and how to get credit): 0898 334 157.

Full realism will be obtained by students calling these numbers live. However, the message is available on the accompanying cassette.

National and Provincial Max Helpline Telemessages

Buying on Credit

Thanks for calling the MAX Helpline – the service designed to help you make the best use of your money.

What do you do when you want to make a major purchase, but don't have the cash to do it?

Well, like most people these days, you buy on credit.

This way you can take the strain out of shopping. But be careful – interest and other charges can make it a painful business. Borrowing money costs money – so use credit wisely and look for the best deals.

Remember, you'll have to pay in the end, so always ask yourself if you really need the goods. If the answer is yes, then ask yourself: How much will I need to borrow? What is the cash price of the goods? How much will I end up paying for them? And, more importantly, can I afford the repayments?

You should shop around for credit, in the same way that you would shop around for anything else. With so many different types of credit on offer, you need a common yardstick to measure the cost of each deal.

This is done by using APR – the Annual Percentage Rate of charge. This is your starting point for finding the cheapest credit. In general: the lower the APR, the better the credit deal.

Check to see how many instalments you will have to make to pay back the loan and what happens to the final figure if you can't afford to pay one or two months.

Don't be pressurised by a salesman. You'll probably find it cheaper to get a loan from a building society or bank to pay for electrical goods, than it is to accept a store's finance scheme.

It's important that you shop around and, if in doubt, seek independent advice.

Thank you for calling the MAX Helpline. I hope our advice was of value.

Borrowing – how and where to get credit

Thanks for calling the Max Helpline – the service designed to help you make the best use of your money.

Borrowing money is an ideal way of spreading the cost of a major purchase. But, be warned it's all too easy to have a spending spree you can't really afford.

Generally, you have to be over 18 to apply for credit, like hire purchase, credit cards and mail order. In some cases, you have to be over 21.

There are many different ways of obtaining credit, so let's just look at the more common methods.

If you're over 18, you can apply for a credit card from the National & Provincial Building Society. With it, you can buy things up to a set limit. You will then be sent a monthly statement showing what you bought and the minimum you must pay back each month. Interest on the money you don't pay back will be charged to your account.

Another way of getting credit is with a charge card. Here, though, you are charged an annual fee to use the card, and you have to settle your whole month's statement in full in one single payment. While there's no interest to pay and no spending limit, you must have enough cash at the end of the month to pay.

Store cards work in a similar way to credit cards and you'll find them very useful if you do a lot of shopping at one shop or store group. However, the APR is higher than that charged by a credit card.

Hire purchase, or HP, is the traditional way to buy on credit. Here, you can take the goods away and pay for them on a weekly or monthly basis. You'll be charged interest and, remember, the goods are not *yours* until you've finished paying for them.

Finally, you may be able to apply for an overdraft facility on your cheque account; though negotiating a loan, from a building society or a bank, may be your cheapest bet.

The most important thing with credit, is to remember that you pay extra for the privilege of borrowing money to buy. So, be wary of interest rates, as they differ enormously. Always read the small print before you sign anything, and shop around for the best deal.

Thank you for calling the MAX Helpline. I hope our advice was of value.

Task 2

This could, if appropriate, be supplemented by any other material on credit – including, perhaps, a range of shopcard leaflets, easily picked up from chainstores.

Task 3

The number of participants depends upon how the group can be split. You can extend the group to six or seven participants by adding one or two 'roadies' (details given below), who, for the convenience of the financing, give their services for free! It is not essential to have one or both 'roadies' if the group is divisible by five or six. Students should elect their own leader of the meeting or allow this to emerge naturally.

Task 4

Dependent upon the outcome of task 3, students should *either* complete individually a loan application form in the name of the person nominated, *or* complete a van hire form.

Both tasks are printed below and should be photocopied for students. A sample loan application form from the National & Provincial Building Society is used. However, any suitable form could be used – particularly if students have actually done the rounds of financial institutions.

Option task (1)
If your group elected to take out a credit agreement, you will need to complete an application form.

This needs to be completed individually in the name of the person you decided was best qualified for a loan. Use your own details (e.g. address), or make them up where appropriate.

Option task (2)
If your group decided, for whatever reason, not to borrow money, you still have problems to face!

The van you bought recently has broken down. It's not a major repair, but the parts won't be available for two days. And tonight you've got a gig.

You need to hire another Ford Transit to transport your equipment just for today.

Using the rates chart below and the insurance proposal form, complete the booking. Remember that Jan drives the band, so for this task, you must take Jan's role. Use your own details (e.g. address) and make up any details necessary (e.g. driving licence number if you're under 17 or don't drive).

PERSONAL LOAN APPLICATION FORM.

Please complete application using BLOCK CAPITAL LETTERS.

Tick ☐ where appropriate.

If you have ever had a Forward Trust Account, please state account number if known.

____

I wish to settle my existing account. YES ☐ NO ☐

PERSONAL DETAILS.

My First Name is ______

My Surname ______ Mr ☐ Mrs ☐ Miss ☐ Ms ☐

My Address ______

______ Postcode ______

Tel. No. ______ I have lived here ______ years.

My previous Adress (if at present address less than two years). ______

______

I lived there for ______ years.

I am the Owner ☐ Joint Owner ☐ Tenant ☐

Living with Parents ☐ Other ☐

I am Married ☐ Single ☐ Widowed ☐ Divorced ☐

Separated ☐

My Date of Birth is ______ I have ______ dependents.

OCCUPATION.

My Job is ______

Employer ______

Employer's Address ______

______

______

Tel. No. ______ I have worked there ______ years.

Previous Employer (if with present Employer less than two years). ______

______

______ I worked there for ______ years.

BANK DETAILS.

I have a Bank Current ☐ Deposit ☐ Savings ☐ account.

My Bank is ______

Branch Address ______

______ I have banked here ______ years.

Bank Sort Code ☐☐·☐☐·☐☐

My Account No(s) ______

______

I hold the following cards: None ☐ Access ☐

Cheque Guarantee ☐

Barclaycard/Visa ☐ American Express ☐

Diner's Club ☐ Trustcard ☐ Other ☐

BUILDING SOCIETY DETAILS.

My Branch's Address is ______

______

My Mortgage Account No. (if applicable) ______

Approx. Balance £ ______ Date Granted ______

My Investment/Savings Account No. ______

Date Opened ______

PERSONAL LOAN INSURANCE PLAN.

Insurance NOT required (tick box) ☐

MONTHLY INCOME AND COMMITMENTS.

Monthly average take home pay	£ ___	Mortgage/ rent/rates	£ ___
Spouse's average take home pay	£ ___	Credit commitments/ HP	£ ___
Child benefit	£ ___	Other commitments (give details)	£ ___
Other income (give details)	£ ___		
______	£ ___	______	£ ___
______	£ ___	______	£ ___
TOTAL	£ ___	TOTAL	£ ___

PERSONAL LOAN (FIXED SUM) APPLICATION.

The amount I require is £ ______
(minimum £500, maximum £7,500)

I will repay my loan over 12 ☐ 24 ☐ 36 ☐ 48 ☐ 60 ☐ months.

I require the loan for ______
(purpose of loan)

I would like the loan to be: Sent direct to my home address ☐

Paid into my National & Provincial Instant Access account ☐

My account number is:

	Account No. (For Office use only.)

DECLARATION.

I enclose my P60 or two weekly/monthly payslips. (All will be returned.)

I propose to pay for my loan by direct debit ☐ payment book ☐ or Standing Order from my Instant Access account ☐ and wish to make my payment on the ______ day of each month.

I/We certify that the information set out above is correct and that I/We are in good health. I/We authorise you to disclose any of the above information in obtaining references or making other enquiries and understand that you may decline this application without stating a reason. I/We understand that the above information may be disclosed to a credit reference agency.

Signature(s) ______

______ Date ______

Applicable to UK residents over 18 years, subject to acceptance.

Please complete and return to Forward Trust Limited, 12 Calthorpe Road, Edgbaston, Birmingham B15 1QZ. Registered Office as above. Registered in England No. 229341.

R2234

HIRE AND DRIVE (Short Period Cover)

Supplementary Proposal

Royal Insurance (U.K.) Ltd

Please complete in BLOCK CAPITALS throughout.

Definition: Hirer means the person who hires the car from the Owner

The Hirer is recommended to acquaint himself with the terms of the Owner's policy as there is a contract of hire between the Hirer and the Owner and any exclusions in the Owner's policy apply equally to the Hirer.

Owner's Name
W. H. BAKER
(CONTRACT HIRE) LTD
Policy Number **RKC 92497**

The undernoted particulars require to be completed by the Hirer and a separate supplementary form to be completed by each individual driver.

Full Name
Please state Mr/Mrs/Miss ________ Age ____

Address ________

Postcode ____

Business or Occupation ________ Hirer's Driving Licence No. ____

Vehicle
Registration Mark of vehicle hired ________

Period of Hire Number of Days ☐ commencing am/pm / /19 Expiring am/pm / /19

If NO please give details

1. Will the motor vehicle be used only for social domestic and pleasure purposes and in connection with the business of the Hirer excluding the carriage of passengers for Hire or reward? Insert YES or NO ☐
2. Are you between 21 and 70 years Insert Yes or NO ☐

If YES please give details

3. Have you or any person who will drive
   (a) had a motoring accident and/or claim during the last 36 calendar months? Insert YES or NO ☐
   (b) been convicted of any motoring offence (other than for parking) or had a licence suspended during the past 5 years or is any such prosecution pending? Insert YES or NO ☐
   (c) any physical or mental defect or infirmity or suffered from diabetes, fits or any heart complaint? Insert YES or NO ☐
   (d) had less than twelve months experience under a full driving licence applicable to the type of vehicle being hired? Insert YES or NO ☐
   (e) ever been convicted of any offence involving dishonesty of any kind e.g. theft, receiving stolen goods? Insert YES or NO ☐
   (f) had any motor vehicle insurance proposal declined or had any motor insurance policy cancelled or special terms imposed? Insert YES or NO ☐

Declaration

Very Important
You are reminded of the need to disclose any facts which the Insurer would take into account in the assessment and acceptance of this proposal.

If you have any doubts as to whether certain facts are relevant please ask your Insurance Broker or local Royal Insurance Office. Failure to disclose all relevant facts may invalidate your cover or may result in the policy not operating fully. Only those persons who have completed a separate supplementary proposal may drive the vehicle.

It is an offence under the Road Traffic Acts to make any false statement

I declare that the information given in this proposal is to the best of my knowledge and belief correct and complete in every detail. I have acquainted myself with the terms exceptions and conditions of the above numbered policy.

Date / /

Signature ....

WELL HILL
SELF·DRIVE LIMITED
COPPER MILL GARAGE, HEATH ROAD, MORRISTON, STANSET SA6 8HL.
TEL: 0791 310020 FAX: 0791 797101

VEHICLE	HIRE	INS.	V.A.T.	TOTAL	PERIOD
	COMMERCIAL VEHICLES				
ESCORT/ASTRA VANS (PETROL)	16.50 66.00	3.00 15.00	2.93 12.15	22.43 93.15	DAILY WEEKLY
DIESEL RATES	17.60 70.40	3.00 15.00	3.09 12.81	23.69 98.21	DAILY WEEKLY
TRANSIT VANS (PETROL)	16.00 70.40	3.00 15.00	2.85 12.81	21.85 98.21	DAILY WEEKLY
DIESEL RATES	19.80 79.20	3.00 15.00	3.42 14.13	26.22 108.33	DAILY WEEKLY
LUTONS & 35 CWT TIPPERS (PETROL)	26.40 105.60	4.00 20.00	4.56 18.84	34.96 144.44	DAILY WEEKLY
MINI BUS 12 SEATER	26.40 105.60	4.00 20.00	4.56 18.84	34.96 144.44	DAILY WEEKLY
15 SEATER	31.00 132.00	6.00 20.00	5.55 22.80	42.55 174.80	DAILY WEEKLY
CARGO BOX – FLAT BED & TIPPERS	48.00 198.00	6.00 25.00	8.10 33.45	62.10 256.45	DAILY WEEKLY
CARGO BOX 19 FOOT WITH TAIL LIFT	55.00 220.00	6.00 25.00	9.15 36.75	70.15 281.75	DAILY WEEKLY
CARGO BOX/SLEEPER CAB/TAIL LIFT	60.00 250.00	6.00 25.00	9.90 41.25	75.90 316.25	DAILY WEEKLY
FORD ORION 1.6 MANUAL/AUTOMATIC	18.00 85.00	3.00 15.00	3.15 15.00	24.15 115.00	DAILY WEEKLY

N.B. A £25.00 CASH DEPOSIT MUST BE TAKEN ON ALL LIGHT VEHICLES.
A MINIMUM RETAINER OF £10.00 MUST BE TAKEN ON MINI BUSES AND CARS TO HOLD BOOKINGS.
A DEPOSIT OF £30.00 PAYABLE ON ALL 7.5 G.V.W. (CARGO'S) . . .

Option task (1)
If your group elected to take out a credit agreement, you will need to complete an application form. This needs to be completed individually in the name of the person you decided was best qualified for a loan. Use your own details (e.g. address), or make them up where appropriate.

Option task (2)
If your group decided, for whatever reason, not to borrow money, you still have problems to face!

The van you bought recently has broken down. It's not a major repair, but the parts won't be available for two days. And tonight you've got a gig. You need to hire another Ford Transit to transport your equipment just for today.

Using the rates chart below and the insurance proposal form, complete the booking. Remember that Jan drives the band, so for this task, you must take Jan's role. Use your own details (e.g. address) and make up any details necessary (e.g. driving licence number if you're under 17 or don't drive).

ASSIGNMENT 9

Making Your Mark

Task 1 Students will need to be provided at the outset with a copy of the conference booking form below.

LET US HELP YOU PLAN THE PERFECT CONFERENCE

Here's a list that you may find useful for organising your conference.

Type of package: Day Delegate ☐ 24 Hour ☐

CONFERENCE DETAILS

Date of Conference: From ________ To ________ Number of Delegates: ________

ROOMS REQUIRED

Meeting

Room Layout ________

Time Required *From* ____ *To* ____

From ____ *To* ____

Smoking/Non smoking ________

Syndicate

Room Layout ________

Time Required *From* ____ *To* ____

From ____ *To* ____

Smoking/Non smoking ________

EQUIPMENT REQUIRED

☐ Flip Chart
☐ Markers
☐ Overhead Projector
☐ TV/Video
☐ 35 mm Slide Projector

☐ Flip Chart
☐ Markers
☐ Overhead Projector
☐ TV/Video
☐ 35 mm Slide Projector

What else will you need to complete your conference/meeting? ________

____

MEALS/REFRESHMENTS

	Coffee	Lunch	Tea	Dinner
Number				
Time				
Location (eg Restaurant)				
Menu required				
Drinks required				
Special requirements (eg Vegetarian Meals)				

ACCOMMODATION DETAILS

Will your delegates require overnight accommodation? ________ *Number and type of bedrooms?* ________

For conferences on a larger scale you may have extra requirements.

Entertainment
☐ Room/Event theming
☐ Gala/Dinner
☐ Dance/Band/Cabaret
☐ Coach tours
☐ Theatre

Publicity
☐ Welcome Posters
☐ Signs/Flags
☐ Photography
☐ Press arrangements

Printing/Stationery
☐ Invitation/Tickets

☐ Programme
☐ Badges
☐ Seating Plan

Administration
☐ Enrolment Desk
☐ Conference Assistants
☐ Secretarial Assistance

☐ Conference Office
☐ Typewriter
☐ Photocopier
☐ Telephone
☐ Telex

Tape transcript
Hello, this is Alison Brown here from Fischer Components.

As you know, our German head office is considering an expansion programme and we've got a number of directors coming over soon and we'd like to book your conference facilities.

Now, these are our requirements:
- We'll be arriving on Friday, the 17 of March;
- and we need the facilities from 9.30 until 5.30 p.m.;
- there'll be 12 delegates and we'd like to use the Abbey Suite meeting room;
- please make sure that you set it out in a 'U' shape beforehand;
- and that there are no ashtrays (you know what a fitness fanatic the Chairman is).

We require the following equipment:
- 1 o.h.p.;
- 1 VHS video recorder (with medium-size TV monitor);
- 1 flipchart and some marker pens;
- and a direct telephone line from the conference room.

We need the following catering:
- coffee and biscuits for 12 people at, shall we say, 11 a.m.;
- lunch for 12 in the restaurant at 12.45. (By the way, we have one Orthodox Jewish director and one vegetarian – so make arrangements for one Kosher and one vegetarian meal.)
- afternoon tea at 3.30 p.m. for 10 – the two councillors will leave after lunch.
- can you serve the tea and coffee in the bar, so that we get a chance to stretch our legs.

Can you confirm these arrangements in writing as soon as possible please, together with a price.

Thank you.

Task 2

The draft should cover the relevant points and avoid references to negative experiences (i.e. divorce and 'only' gaining silver medal.) Tone should be welcoming and warm, emphasising positive links and future prospects.

Tasks 3 and 4

The tasks are linked and should stress students' ability to be assertive, yet diplomatic. In each case, Laurie should try to persuade the other person towards a particular course of action, without giving away principles, but being prepared to compromise. It is acceptable for the other person to be obstreperous but care should be taken not to allow the exchanges to become a slanging match.

If positive outcomes are stressed beforehand, this should not occur. Pairs will need to carry out their exchanges uninterrupted. (It will probably not be possible for the exchanges to be taped unless the class is very small.)

This assignment presents the opportunity for students to discuss their experiences, and their attempts at persuasion in what amounts to a debriefing session. Which tactics worked for them here? Appealing to reason? Appealing to sense of being fellow Europeans? Emotional appeal? Blackmail? Being reasonable? Being heavyhanded, etc.?

Such discussion will also be a useful introduction to the concept of self- and group evaluation, whether or not the students will be attempting the level 3 assignments.

ASSIGNMENT 10

Up to Your Ears

This assignment is designed to provide experience of decision making and communicating, in a variety of ways under time constraints.

As such, it is a complex assignment, which should not be given to students early on in their course. Nor should it be given before students are familiar with the techniques of memo writing, formal letter writing and taking notes from the telephone.

The assignment may be adapted, with the suggestions on p. 27, to upgrade it to a Level 3 assignment.

Tasks 1 and 2 are intertwined and should be completed together. Students will need a continuous period of 75–90 minutes to complete this. It is not fair, or realistic, to split the sessions for these tasks.

Task 1 requires response to the written material in the assignment, plus a copy of the diary page. Task 2 requires listening to two tape messages and making two phone calls.

Call 1 should be made approximately 15 mins into the assignment, and Call 2 about 30 minutes in.

Because the assignment attempts to replicate the atmosphere and conditions of office-work, it is essential that:
- students work entirely on their own;
- material is available for them at their desk;
- phone calls are received or made in a realistic way.

Ideally, students should be able to use a telephone system with recording facilities in a workshop/model office situation. Realistically, this may not be possible in your centre. As an alternative, make a number of copies of tapes (say one per four students) which can be played through headphones when students are ready. Students should also have access to tape recorders to use when ready – preferably in private and without having to queue to use them.

Students will need the following stationery supplied – telephone message sheets, memo sheets, company headed notepaper. These are provided ready for cutting and distribution. Students should not be told which stationery should be used for which response.

It is very useful for students to have a clock in the room, set for 09.00 at the outset of the assignment. If you cannot arrange this, give the students time-checks every 15 minutes.

Task 1

There is no specific order of priorities. However, the following must be borne in mind:
- it is essential to move the car immediately (if necessary, by asking someone else to do it);
- the MD must be phoned by 09.50;
- Dixon Photocopiers must be phoned early on with a request for attention a.s.a.p.

Task 2

Transcripts

1 To be played approximately 15 minutes into task 1.

Hello. Is that Starlight Video? My name's Terri Mitchell. I rented two videos, distributed by you from Well Hill Video in River Town last week. When I went to return them, I found that the shop had gone out of business. The letterbox was sealed, so I couldn't push them through.

The tapes say 'Property of Starlight Video' on them. If I post them back to you, will you refund my postage costs?

You will? O.K. My address is 4 Rose Bank, River Town, WB2 9ML and my name's Terri Mitchell. Goodbye.

2 To be played about 30 minutes into task 1.

Hello, Oliver Smith here, company solicitor. Can I speak to Sylvie Lehmann, please? You what? Lehmann? Oh, I'm sorry. She's on holiday! Oh blast! OK, you're her assistant, are you?.

Well listen, we've got a problem. Some of the videos we sent to Town & Country Newsagents were packaged wrongly – kids' cartoons in feature-film cases, you know the sort of thing. Yeah, well – wait for it – the worst is that four adult horror movies, rated Restricted 18, were packaged in children's cartoon cases. Well, Town & Country sold four of these to parents as children's birthday presents. When they were played, the parents were furious.

And as you can imagine, Town & Country have gone up the wall – how many more have they got in stock etc., etc? Now then, two of their directors are coming in at two o'clock, and I would very much like someone from PR to help smoothe the way. Come down at 1.45, will you, so that we can discuss things beforehand? Oh, and contact Wesley Rees in Packaging. Explain the mess and get him to come with you.

Task 3

Discussion should range over the possibilities of presentation for each set of figures. Groups should decide on appropriate format and a variety of presentation.

Task 4

Graph paper should be available.

TELEPHONE MESSAGE

From:

Date:

Tel. no.:

Time:

MEMORANDUM

From:

Ref:
Subject:

To:

Date:

STARLIGHT VIDEO

Hollywood House, Elstree Boulevard, Yoretown
ME2 3PK

Tel. 0673 588352 Fax. 0673 456000

Managing Director: Jan Poliakoff B.Sc. FCA

Registered in England No. 1417709

The assignment may be upgraded to level 3 by substituting the following tasks in line with level 3 objectives:

Omit tasks 3 and 4. Replace the meeting in task 3 with the meeting outlined in task 2, phone call no. 2 – the meeting with the directors of Town & Country Newsagents. Replace task 4 with an evaluation of the learning process in the assignment.

Students should receive the following for level 3.

Task 3

After lunch, you have to prepare for the meeting you've been called to by the company solicitor with the directors of Town & Country Newsagents (task 2).

This meeting will need to be role played by six people: two directors; one company solicitor; the personal assistant(s) and Wesley Rees.

- The class will split into a group/groups of five or six. When the roles have been decided, the two directors will need to prepare their case and the three or four Starlight employees their case.

  No legal knowledge is required for this meeting. But students will need to think about the likely viewpoints of the people involved, and to prepare their case on this basis. They will be assessed on:
  - the quality of their case;
  - common sense, tact and diplomacy;
  - their demonstration of a real willingness to suggest solutions to the problem;
  - their support of their colleagues;
  - non-verbal communication.

Task 4

This assignment has involved students in carrying out a number of communication tasks under the additional pressure of time limits.

- This task is an evaluation of the work carried out to date. They now have to consider:
  - how effective they think the written and oral communications they have initiated are;
  - how effective the meeting was, and their own and others' performance in it;
  - how they responded to the pressure of time-constraints on the decision making process.
- Write a brief, informal report for your tutor.

ASSIGNMENT 11

Right-Price Records

Task 1 Students should copy out address at heading. Memo should follow format provided.

Task 2 Plain A4 paper is needed. Poster should meet criteria given in task, but need not be artistic. Clear communication is paramount.

Task 3 Appropriate costing is £5.10 per scc. In other words, an advertisement measuring either 10 lines × single column or 5 lines × double column width costs £51.00, plus VAT.

Task 4 Adequate taping facilities need to be made available for those who do not have facilities at home. This task could produce some very good and original tapes. Emphasise the crucial timing. Class assessment of tapes should be positive and encouraging, in order to derive maximum benefit from next task.

Task 5 Honesty and openness should be encouraged for this task. Students need to evaluate their own strengths and weaknesses, with supporting comments from others.

ASSIGNMENT 12

Wellwishers

This assignment asks students to consider the pros and cons of assembly line production through a simulated activity using greetings cards.

The assignment moves towards discussing management theories of motivation, but can be completed with very little theoretical input.

Much of the detail is in the introductory material, and students should be encouraged to read this carefully – particularly for the implied attitudes of Wellwishers' current management.

Task 1 Careful reading will produce useful notes.

Task 2 Each group of students should be given photocopies of the instructions for greetings card assembly. Each group will also need the following:

- a copy of flower patterns to be cut as desired;
- one sheet coloured A4 card;
- scissors;
- six sheets × A4 paper trimmed on both length and width by 2 cm;
- six envelopes (approx 15 cm × 22 cm);
- gum;
- clear plastic/cellophane bags, e.g. food bags on a roll;
- a small cardboard box, e.g. shoe or shirt box;
- a selection of marker pens.

Task 3 You are asked to lead this discussion. Each student should be asked in turn to present amendments to the assembly line method. It will be useful to cover the points mentioned as sub-headings for the notes in task 1. A key question which should emerge concerns the artistic skill needed as inscriber and floral arranger – can these skills be taught, or is a certain flair a prerequisite in order to complete these tasks to the customers' satisfaction?

Task 4 A formal report is not required here. However, students should reflect seriously on their own and others' work, and detail their responses accordingly.

Extension studies If students are interested in this area of study, it might be useful to look at the industrial psychology work of McGregor, Herzberg, Maslow and Mayo.

Instructions for making greetings cards

Before you begin, decide as a team whether the finished card is to stand

or

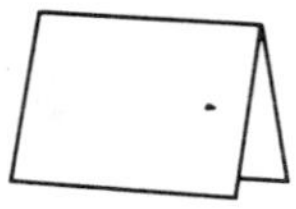

Floral Arrangers
Fold card in half.
Stick on paper flowers in an attractive arrangement of your choice.

Inscribers
Fold paper in half.
On the *inside* page inscribe one of the following:

Happy Birthday
Best Wishes
In Sympathy
Thank you

Trace and cut out as many as you need.

Attach paper insert to card with a little glue along fold.

Trace and cut out as many as you need.